Published May 2021
Published by Indies United Publishing House, LLC

Cover art & interior artwork by Leslie A. Piggott

ISBN: 978-1-64456-263-5
Library of Congress Control Number: 2021931411

INDIES UNITED PUBLISHING HOUSE, LLC
P.O. BOX 3071
QUINCY, IL 62305-3071
www.indiesunited.net

Dedication

To Brad, Abby, and Simon: thanks for supporting my creative endeavors.
I love you so much, forever and always.

For Luiska,

Thank you for your support of my new creative outlet! I am so thankful for your friendship. Your kindness and compassion for people is inspiring.

♡ Leslie

Table of Contents

Poems in the Pandemic

Written and Illustrated by Leslie A. Piggott

Before and After

Life
Once so carefree
So innocent.
When the unexpected
Was exciting
And mysterious.
When it seemed that far past
The sky—was the LIMIT.
That there were no boundaries.
Now
Seems so fragile
So unprotected.
Where the unexpected is
Terrifying.
Where fears are running high
And WALLS continually go up
In the name of safety.
When hope is hard
And peace seems out of reach.
Love is steadfast
Hope will persevere
And Faith will endure
For God is with us.

Seeking Hope

God
Waiting in heaven.
Souls
Returning home
Daily
By the thousands.
When Lazarus died,
Jesus wept.
Who weeps now?
Loneliness
Feels fully tangible.
They that hope in the Lord,
Shall renew their strength.
My strength wanes.
Father God,
Hear our cry.
Heal your sons and daughters.
Restore our hope.
Forgive our weakness.
You walk
Beside us
Before us
Behind us.

Crying for Comfort

Help us
To seek you
We are
Lost
In the wilderness
Of disease.
May we see Your Light
And find Comfort.

Healing

Prayers are raised: Continually, Constantly, Pleadingly.
Struggling
For clarity.
How   Why   When...
As the days
Count higher
Alongside the deaths
The endless infection
Rages
Its hosts: Equal opportunity
Its victims, much less so.
The world: Lush, Green, Alive.
Its habitants: Cowering, Gasping, Questioning.
Much seems uncertain
Life, more precious
Time, more endless, yet somehow
Hanging from some unknown
Precipice.
As we grasp for hope
Our dreams feeling somewhat
Shattered,
We plead with Our Creator
To restore our world.

Wandering

Subconsciously
Perceiving
Guilt.
An unknown grievance
Must be righted.
How did we get here?
Trying to find Home
Yet always being there.
Constant uncertainty.
Constant monotony.
Is the end near?
Is it the end that we seek?
Dichotomy arises.
Some fight for life,
Some search for answers,
All desire peace.

Springtime in Pandemic

Gentle rains washing in hope.
The NEWS, like a quicksand
Of ever-rising numbers.
Spring: Synonymous with new life,
New Beginnings,
Yet, this Spring, morbidity looms
As we hunker down.
What fear looms on the horizon?
What do we fear more:
Disease, or uncertainty?
The world longs for renewal
For hope
For evidence of restoration.
When will we arrive there?
We are on a journey to the unknown.
We must arrive at this destination
Without taking
A
Single
Step.

Finding Faith

Each morning
Faith renewed
The day begins
Seemingly unmarred by tragedy.
Yet
One can only ignore
The new reality
For so long.
The virus,
Unfazed by modern medicine,
Races through our communities
Leaving victims by the thousand in its wake.
God of our fathers,
Our faith hangs
Threadbare.
Days pass
Without holding obvious meaning.
We grasp for answers,
For understanding.
We strain for victory,
Struggle, for insight.
Seeking balance

Desiring relief.

Our hearts are consoled by yours.

Your compassion is with us.

This season will end.

Hope will outlast fear.

Faith will see us through.

Seeking Light

When this ends
Who will remain
Untouched,
Unchanged?
Or without sacrifice?
Isolating
Yet uniting.
Hope looms in the distance
Sometimes skating by
In a brief, flicker of light.
Unquenched by the surmounting darkness
Of lives lost.
The Light cannot,
Will Not
Be Overcome.
Faith
Perhaps misplaced at times
In things that cannot sustain,
Seeks the Light,
Satiated and renewed.

But Still

Overwhelming bleakness
Looms around me.
Straining for hope
Searching for something tangible.
My prayers are heard.
This I KNOW.
Thunder roars.
Despair looks for a foothold.
But still.
I will not be shaken.
Nor will I be moved.
The disease circulates,
Spreads,
And sometimes,
Conquers.
But still.
God walks with us.
Holds us.
Knows us.
No matter the outcome,
We are still God's.

14

Finding Connection

Joining together
Across miles
Hearts connected
Hearts entwined
Feeling seen, even touched
Without making physical contact.
God crosses these boundaries.
God's connection of love
Never broken
God's arms of compassion
Never missing.
We are not forsaken
Not forgotten.
We are loved.
We are held.
We are known.

Moments of Despair

Oh God,
I want to believe you hear me.
I want to feel that you are comforting me.
I want to feel something other than alone.
Sweet Jesus,
I feel despair.
I feel a bit lost.
I don't see your hand,
Yet I know it's there.
Is there no rescue crew?
When does this suffering end?
How do I pray for help?
Where do I find relief?

Standing

We stand,
Where the jokes have ended,
Longing to laugh.
We dream
Of times when we were together,
Wishing they were now.
We rise,
Going through the motions,
Hoping for good news.
We gaze,
At the world around us,
Wondering where we stand.

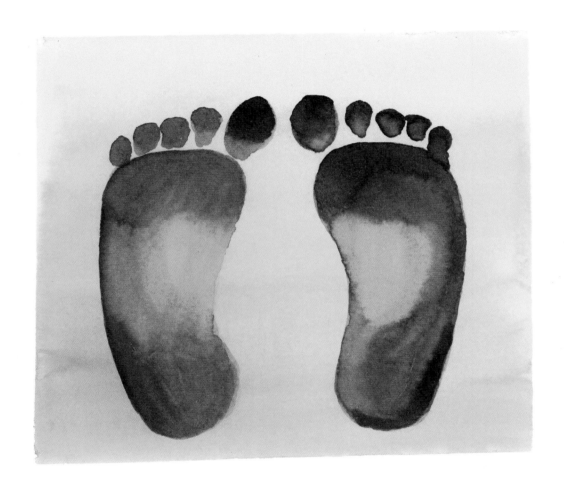

Redefining

Where is the world that I once called home?
Where is the stability I so often took for granted?
I have long-since surpassed the idea of waking from an unfathomable nightmare.
This is not a novel with a plot of a dystopian future.
This is my new reality.
Things once certain feel precarious.
This is not a disruption.
It is a new course.
While disease rages and emotions run high,
The world is experiencing a new tack.
May we forge ahead together.
May we see what was broken and find new ways to fix it.
May we open our eyes to the injustices that we've refused to see before.
May we be the LOVE that the word needs
Instead of the judgment with which it's already been filled.

Restoration

O Lord, where do we see your vision?
Where do we find your joy?
Where do we look for justice?
Where do we turn for hope?
Open our hearts to your will.
Open our ears to your dreams.
Align our goals with your calling.
Restore our hope for tomorrow.
Let joy sing again.

Travel

Some days the road seems longer than usual.
Some days the uncertainty of the future feels insurmountable.
Some days my significance appears insignificant.
Some days my desire to masquerade as an ostrich in the
desert is hard to overcome.
As fearful thoughts continually circle around me,
Where do I find refuge?
You say, "Joy still comes in the morning,"
But when does the morning come?
Am I allowing moments of mornings to pass me by
As I tread in my pool of fear?
Am I searching for answers that do not exist?
I long to have unshakeable faith, but feel myself growing
weary.
May the Spirit of hope move like a strong wind.
May I draw comfort in the wishes of a new season.
May I see the heart of God in the world that is my home.

Road of Life

We have walked the road of life thinking that the road will always be recognizable.

We have taken comfort in "knowing" that at least the road will always be a road. It might be hilly or windy or muddy, but it is still a road.

When we awake to discover that we are no longer walking down a road, but now navigating through stormy water, we panic. "Where is our road? Where is the life we have always known? How do we restore that?"

Maybe instead we should ask how we adapt to our new setting. The old has gone. The new does not have to be bad. Maybe the stormy water is ushering in a new wave that is better than the road we long to rebuild.

Anguish

Sitting on my bed
Crying
Not wanting to laugh
Not wanting to cry
Trying so hard to be in the moment.
Trying to see where hope lies.
Feeling overwhelmed by the weight of tomorrow.
Unable to enjoy today.
Please, Jesus, send relief.

Floundering

Inward restlessness.

Outward joyfulness.

Unreconciled turmoil.

Incomplete dreams.

What do you desire?

What do you seek?

Where do you turn when it feels like love is not enough?

What do you pray for when you don't know what you want?

Who can answer the questions you don't want to ask?

Perspective

In the beginning,
We were naïve,
Uninformed.
Maybe even ignorant.
Fears ran high.
The unknown and endless uncertainty fueled our hysteria.
The number of questions
Smothered
The few answers we could find.
Our trust plummeted.
We wondered where our new equilibrium would settle.
IF it would settle.
We joked.
We criticized.
We cried for unity
While demonizing anyone with differences.
We longed for restoration.
For something that reminded us of "normal".
Will we discover patience?
Will we find peace?
Will we Love?

Tunnel Vision

People speak of a light at the end of the tunnel.
Sometimes it feels like I can't even see the tunnel,
Let alone whether or not it has a light.
Faith is knowing that the light is there, even if unseen.
Life feels like uphill running right now.
That we just keep pushing up and onward
Towards the peak,
But it just keeps getting higher.
Just need more patience,
More perseverance,
More endurance.

29

The Language of Love

What language did the angels speak
The night our Savior came?
What people understood their song
That rose above the earth?
At Pentecost, the Holy Spirit came,
Bringing the good news in such a way
That all who heard could know.
When the angels sang of our Savior's birth,
What language hit each ear?
Did they speak with judgment
With voices filled with scorn?
Did they sing condemning lyrics
That made men fall in shame?
While I cannot say, for I was not there,
I think I will believe,
That the angels sang that all could hear
And they sang their words in Love.

Love Came Down at Christmas

Love came down at Christmas.
Christmas 2020.
In a year filled with uncertainty,
Fear,
Doubt,
Loss of trust,
And isolation,
Love still came.
Love is present.
Love is the light shining in the darkness.
Shining in each of us.
We have seen life challenged this year.
We have seen judgment on nearly every front.
We have endured pain.
We have persevered through trial after trial.
We have found ways to come together
While remaining apart.
Love came down at Christmas,
2000 years ago.
But Love never left.
Love remains
It is steadfast,
Breaking through the darkness that has challenged our days.
May we see the Love of Christmas
May we seek Love and find Hope.

Unrelenting Judgment

Some days
The perceived judgment I feel
Almost outweighs my fear of getting sick.
So many battles are raging:
Physically against a viral pandemic,
Socially against accepted boundaries,
Emotionally against our psyches as we strive for comfort.
Agonizing over what has been lost
While feeling calloused by the high death tolls.
Can you strain for balance?
We have built a dam—
An effort to keep the virus out.
Each of us
Scrambling to avoid the leaks
Which grow in number daily.
As the pressure builds,
We try to remain resolute,
Uncompromising.
Relief feels close
But still out of reach.

Seeking Relief

Bend, don't break.

Persevere.

Endure.

How far can we bend?

How long must we persevere?

Where does relief reside?

Like children on a road trip,

We ask, "Are we there yet?"

What does "there" look like?

As the pandemic rolls on,

Without any sign of dampening,

It feels like we're failing.

Like we must be making constant missteps.

Life, once taken for granted,

Feels paused,

Yet rushing on.

We long for contact,

For something to break free.

We grasp for hope,

Continually feeling

Like it's out of reach.

Yet we are not abandoned.

We are not forgotten.
We are held.
We are known.
We will one day gather safely,
Our joy renewed, restored.

Division

Our world feels foreign.
Changed.
We question everything.
We trust little.
The designations of "Haves" and "Have-Nots"
Are redefined.
Like a scarlet A,
The mark of disease
Is not forgotten.
We continually speak of kindness,
But look with scorn
On those who are struck sick.
No reward awaits those who are unscathed.
May our cry for Unity be pure.
May we join together with love.

God Is Present

Child of God
Lift your head
Don't despair
Your cries are heard
The discomfort of the present
Will not last forever.
God is still with us.
Your pain is not unseen.
Your grief is not unnoticed.
You are not forgotten.
You've endured the unimaginable.
You've experienced tremendous loss.
You seek comfort amidst your isolation.
God knows.
God hears.
God is present.

Refocus

How did we get here?

When did we forget who we are?

When did we stop loving our neighbor?

Who knew staying home was so hard?

We say, "there's no I in TEAM"

While constantly looking out for #1.

We wear our "Be Kind" t-shirts

While rolling our eyes

And calling each other stupid.

Our lives a surreal dichotomy

Of self-righteousness and spirituality.

We cry that God has been pushed from our narrative

While judging others' values as less.

We've redefined "neighbor" as our replicas,

Turning our backs on those who differ.

Can we recenter and remember who is welcome at the table?

Real Life Pain

New life experiences
Singing church hymns
Tears in my eyes
As notes choke out.
Seeing my child
Eyes wide with concern.
Why is Mom crying?
Pain, stemming from loss
From change
From witnessing callous disregard,
Grows deeper daily.
Overwhelming desire for relief
For the world to right its course.
How much more can we endure?

Breaking Point

There is a brokenness
That is breaking me.
Conflict, death, and unrest
The joy I seek
Continually out of reach.
Is the desire to be right so strong?
Where is love hiding?
Am I part of the hate?
What resolution is coming?
Can we find the love we've abandoned?
Will we see past our hurt?
Will we find good in our neighbor?
We must get up.
We must not wallow.
We can work together while being apart.
Hope has not fallen.
Love is within us.
We will persevere.

Held

Remember
The God who parted the waters,
Who shielded youths from the fire,
Who shut the lions' mouths
Is with you too.
The God who brought down giants,
Who healed the blind and the lame,
Who brought the dead to life
Has not deserted you.
From water to wine
To grave to life
God knows you.
God hears you.
God sees you.
Let yourself be held.

Prayer for the Pandemic

In the midst of WIDESPREAD suffering,
I pray that my love would be more
WIDESPREAD
In the face of endless infection,
I pray that my compassion would know no end.
As our time of quarantine increases,
So may too my generosity to my neighbor.